KNIGHTS TEMPLAR THE FELLOW SOLDIERS OF CHRIST

KNIGHTS TEMPLAR KIDS BOOK CHILDREN'S MEDIEVAL BOOKS

In this book, we're going
to talk about the Knights
Templar in Medieval times.
So, let's get right to it!

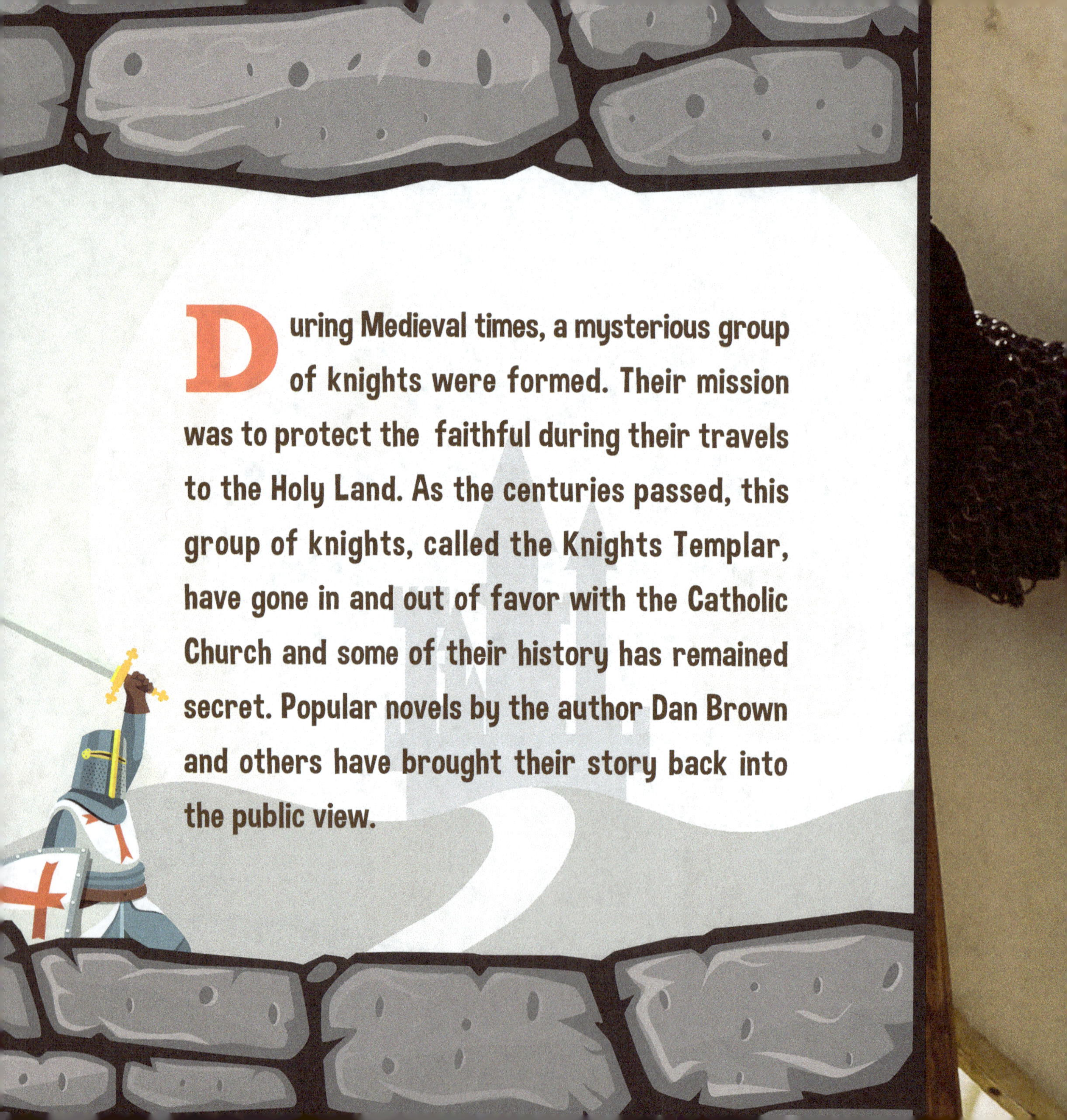

During Medieval times, a mysterious group of knights were formed. Their mission was to protect the faithful during their travels to the Holy Land. As the centuries passed, this group of knights, called the Knights Templar, have gone in and out of favor with the Catholic Church and some of their history has remained secret. Popular novels by the author Dan Brown and others have brought their story back into the public view.

WHO WERE
THE KNIGHTS
TEMPLAR?

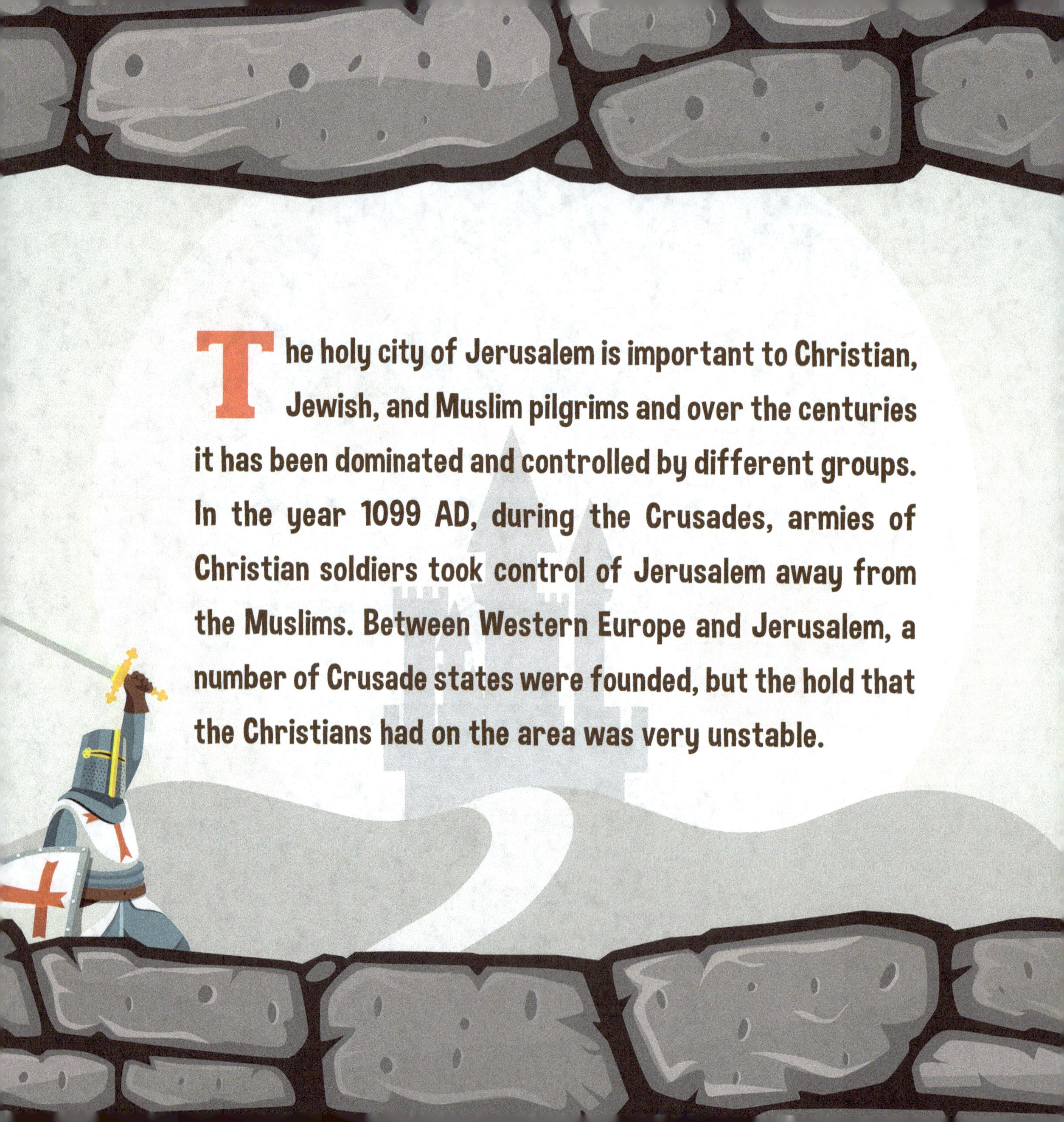

The holy city of Jerusalem is important to Christian, Jewish, and Muslim pilgrims and over the centuries it has been dominated and controlled by different groups. In the year 1099 AD, during the Crusades, armies of Christian soldiers took control of Jerusalem away from the Muslims. Between Western Europe and Jerusalem, a number of Crusade states were founded, but the hold that the Christians had on the area was very unstable.

JERUSALEM

ROAD TO HOLY LAND

Many of the Crusaders went back to their homes after the Crusades were over so the areas weren't being defended. Because of this, Christian pilgrims who wanted to visit and worship in the Holy Land had to journey through dangerous Muslim-controlled areas and they were often robbed and sometimes killed.

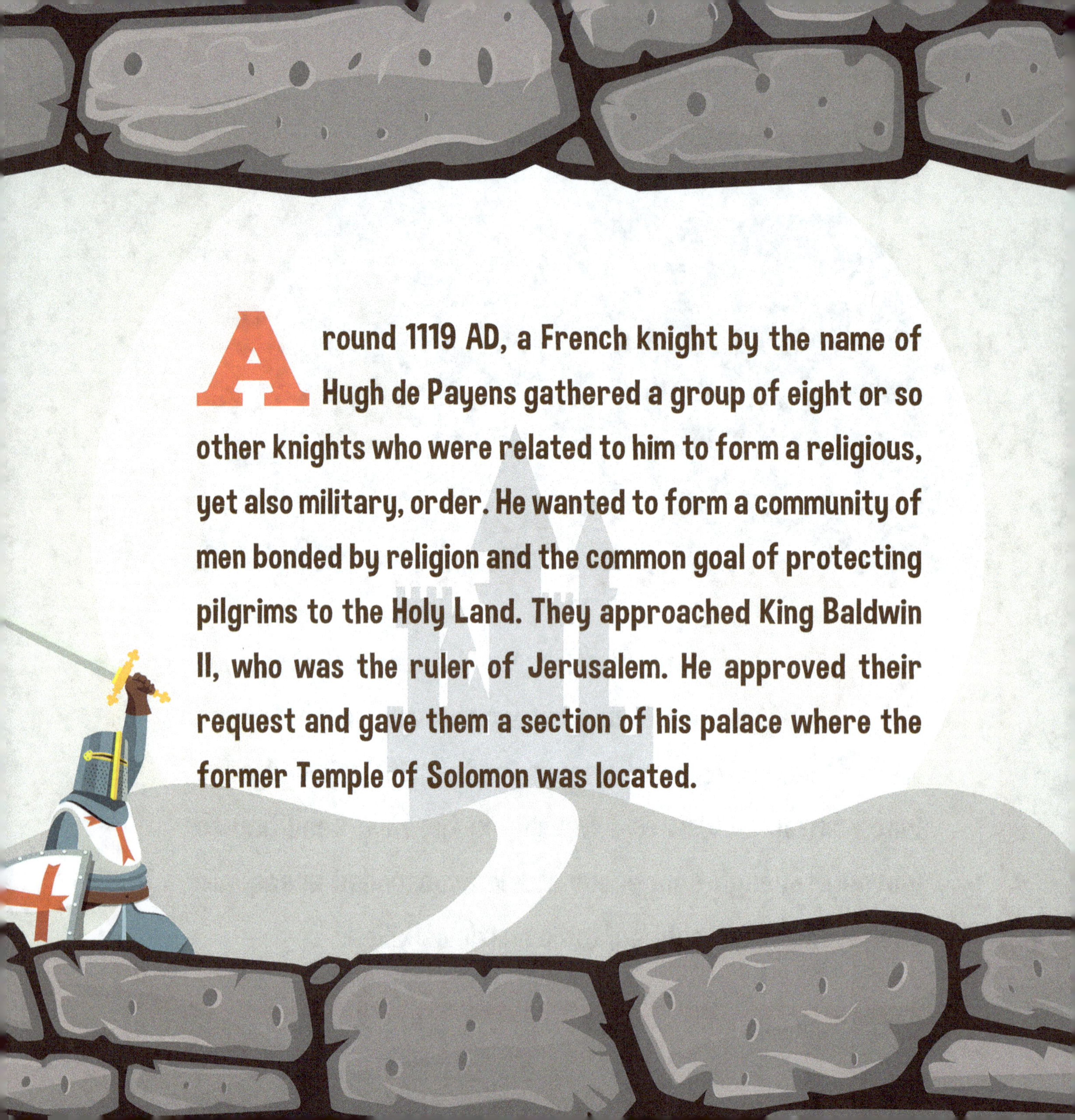

round 1119 AD, a French knight by the name of Hugh de Payens gathered a group of eight or so other knights who were related to him to form a religious, yet also military, order. He wanted to form a community of men bonded by religion and the common goal of protecting pilgrims to the Holy Land. They approached King Baldwin II, who was the ruler of Jerusalem. He approved their request and gave them a section of his palace where the former Temple of Solomon was located.

HUGH DE PAYENS

TEMPLAR'S FIRST EMBLEM

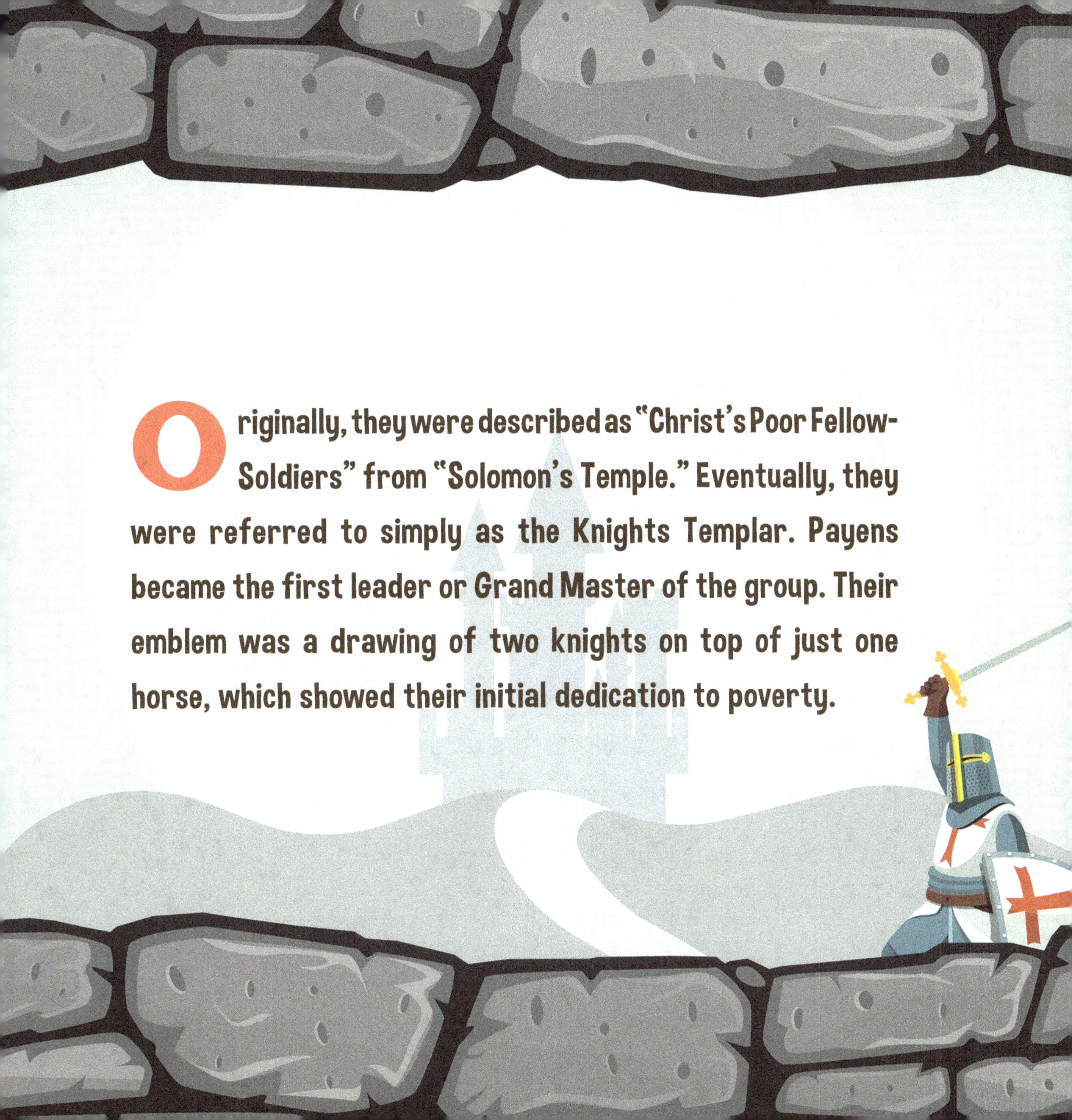

riginally, they were described as "Christ's Poor Fellow-Soldiers" from "Solomon's Temple." Eventually, they were referred to simply as the Knights Templar. Payens became the first leader or Grand Master of the group. Their emblem was a drawing of two knights on top of just one horse, which showed their initial dedication to poverty.

ENDORSEMENT FROM THE CATHOLIC CHURCH

At the beginning, the organization of the Knights Templar was criticized by the Catholic clergy. In 1127, Payens traveled around Europe to meet with wealthy nobles to gain money and endorsements for their important cause. They were given further credibility almost a decade after they had begun, when the Catholic Church formally provided an endorsement for them at the Council of Troyes in the year 1129. Around that time, they were also recognized by Bernard of Clairvaux, who was a well-known abbot in France. An abbot is the leader of a monastery of monks.

BERNARD OF CLAIRVAUX

Bernard may have been commissioned to write the new rules for their order after the Council of Troyes. He later authored a text that lent support to their cause called *In Praise of the New Knighthood*, which was published in 1136.

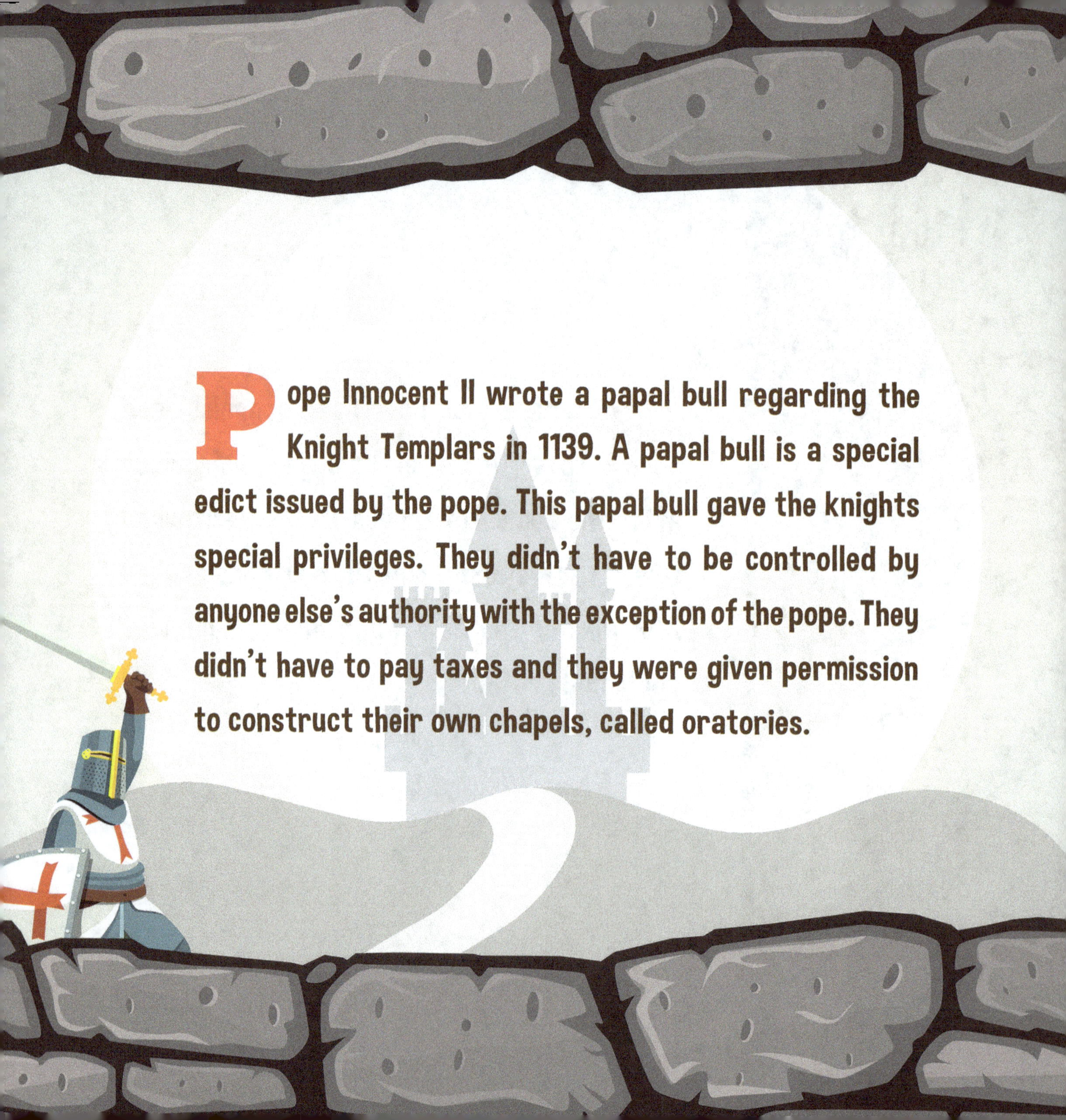

Pope Innocent II wrote a papal bull regarding the Knight Templars in 1139. A papal bull is a special edict issued by the pope. This papal bull gave the knights special privileges. They didn't have to be controlled by anyone else's authority with the exception of the pope. They didn't have to pay taxes and they were given permission to construct their own chapels, called oratories.

POPE INNOCENT II

MONK

WHAT RULES DID THE KNIGHTS TEMPLAR LIVE BY?

The Knights Templar followed rules that were similar to those of the Benedictine monks, especially as followed by the Cistercians, a group of monks dedicated to living their lives as St. Benedict did. The Knights Templar renounced the world's evils just as other monks did. They also made oaths that they would live their lives ruled by chastity, obedience, and poverty.

They participated in certain prayers and hymns at dedicated times of the day called the canonical hours, such as 9 am, 12 noon, and 3 pm. The prayers were called the divine office. They also adhered to the same fasts and ceremonial vigils as those of monasteries. They had a special reverence for the Virgin Mary. They lived together, had a dormitory they shared, and ate their meals at a common table. They didn't swear or drink alcohol and didn't participate in gambling. They weren't cloistered, which simply means that they weren't sheltered from the outside world as many orders of monks and nuns were.

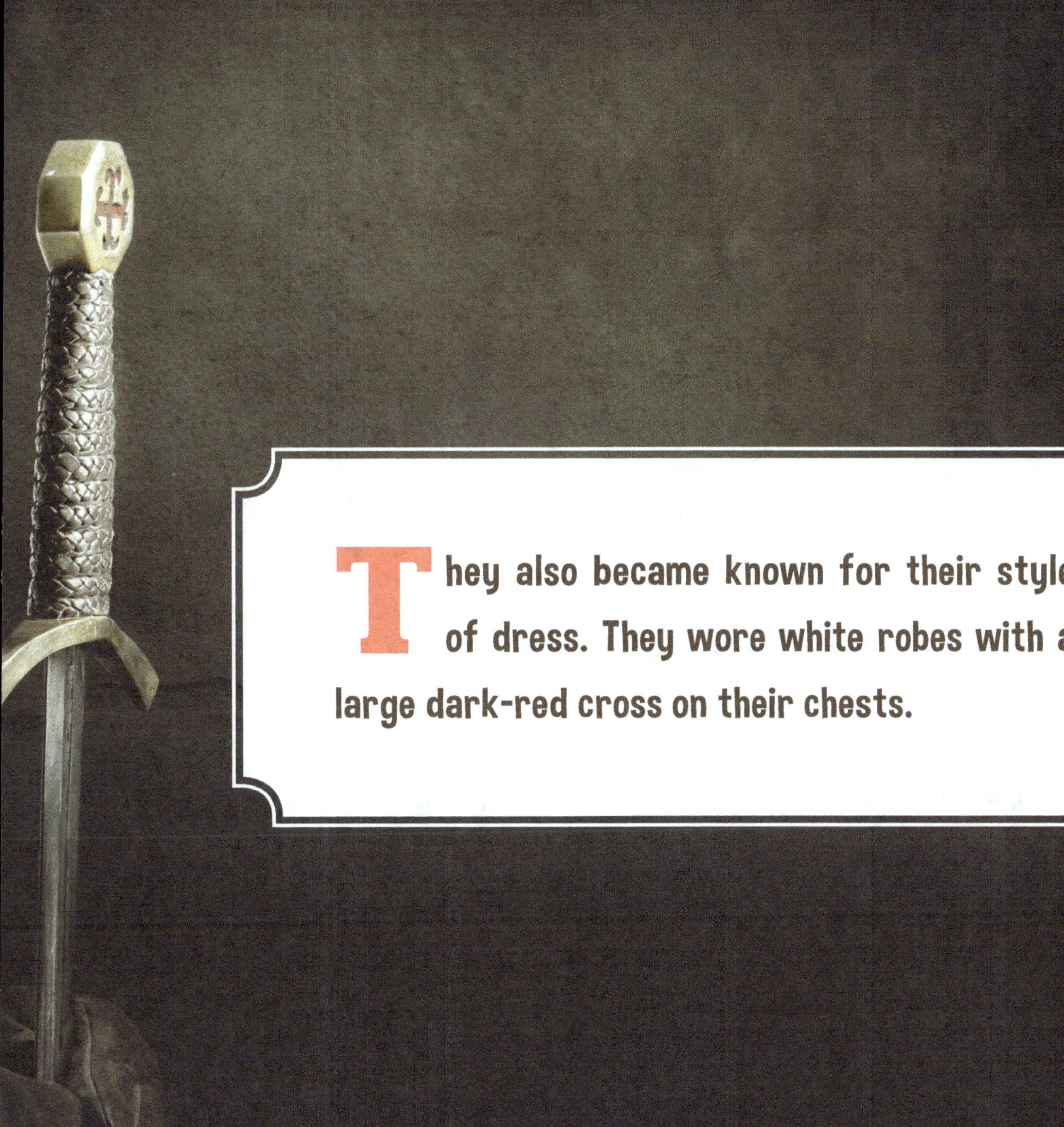

They also became known for their style of dress. They wore white robes with a large dark-red cross on their chests.

THE INFLUENCE
OF THE KNIGHTS
TEMPLAR

TEMPLAR CASTLE

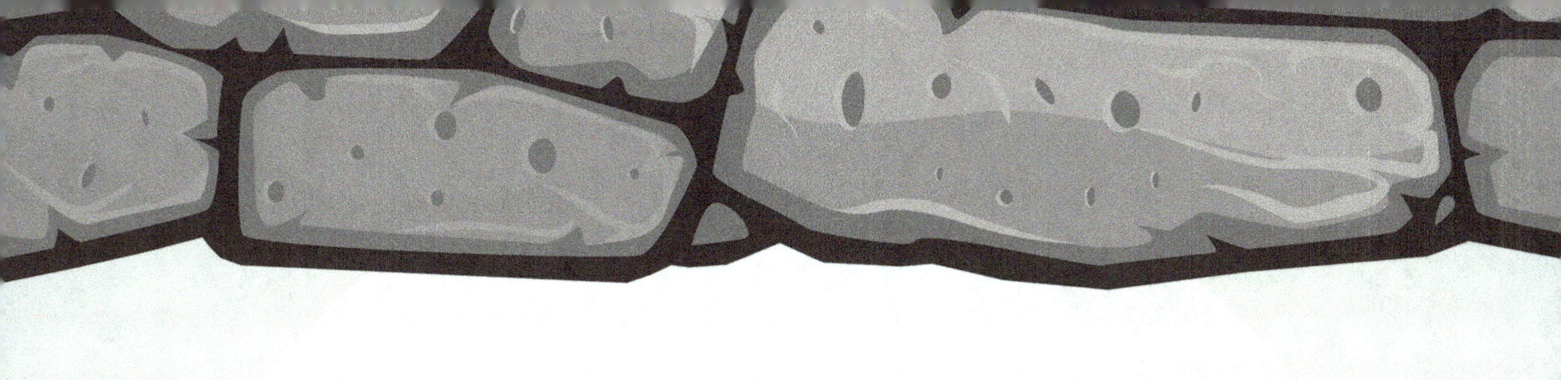

Over the two centuries that the organization of the Knights Templar was at its height, it's estimated that there were eventually 160,000 members and 20,000 were knights. Despite their initial vow of poverty, as an organization they became very wealthy and influential throughout Christian Europe. They set up one of the first banking systems. Pilgrims could deposit money in their home countries and then withdraw the money to sustain them as they visited the Holy Land.

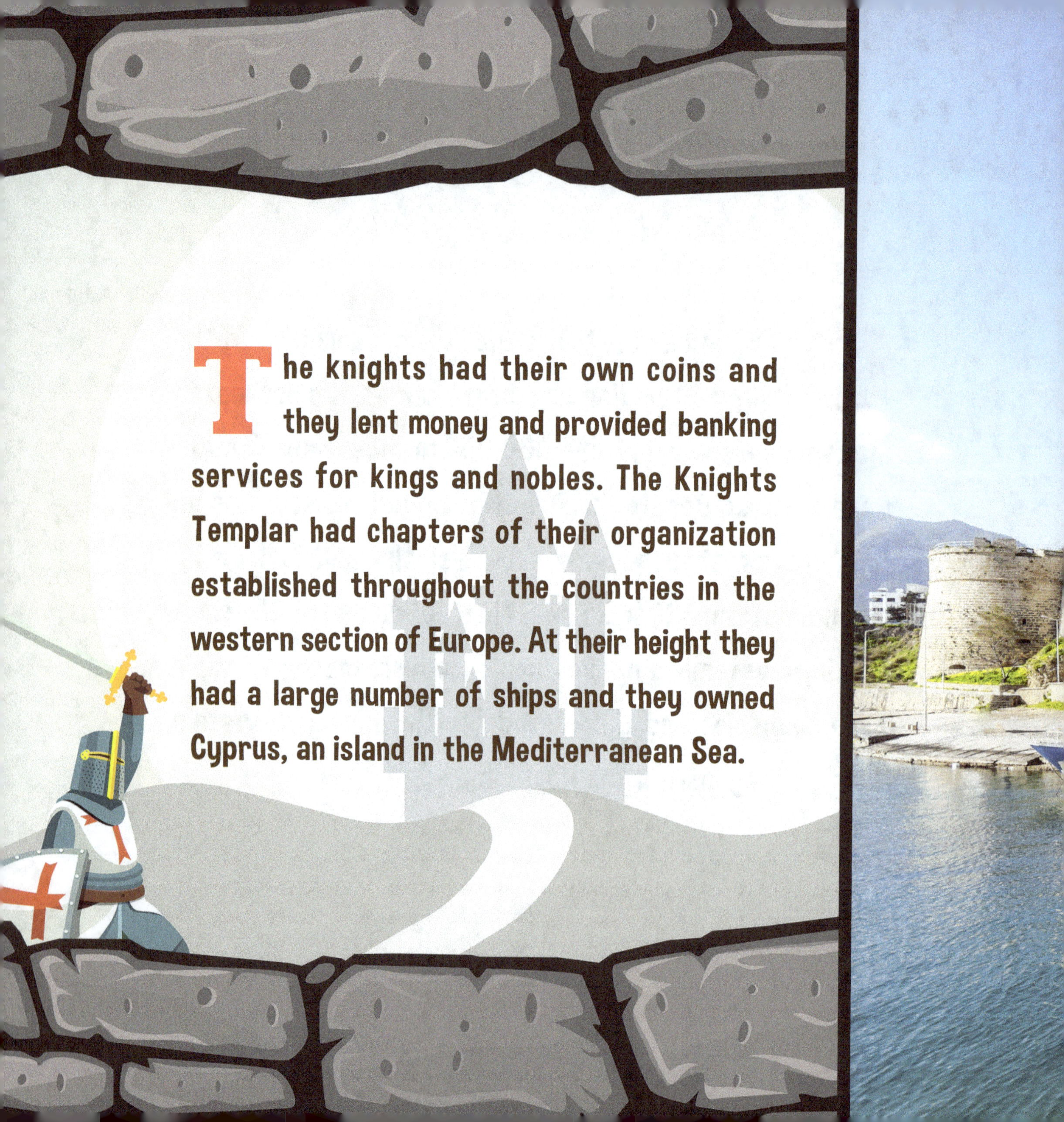

The knights had their own coins and they lent money and provided banking services for kings and nobles. The Knights Templar had chapters of their organization established throughout the countries in the western section of Europe. At their height they had a large number of ships and they owned Cyprus, an island in the Mediterranean Sea.

CYPRUS

CRUSADER
ARMOR

NEW MISSIONS FOR THE KNIGHTS TEMPLAR

As time went on, the order expanded its duties from protecting pilgrims to defending the Crusader states that had been founded in the Holy Land. They were known for their courage and skill in battle. Driven by their religious faith, they were fierce warriors throughout the years of the Crusades. Their principles forbade them to retreat from battle unless they were hopelessly outnumbered.

Their style of fighting provided a model for other subsequent military orders. They also built many beautiful castles for their military bases throughout Europe.

PONFERRADA
TEMPLAR CASTLE

THE FALL OF THE KNIGHTS TEMPLAR

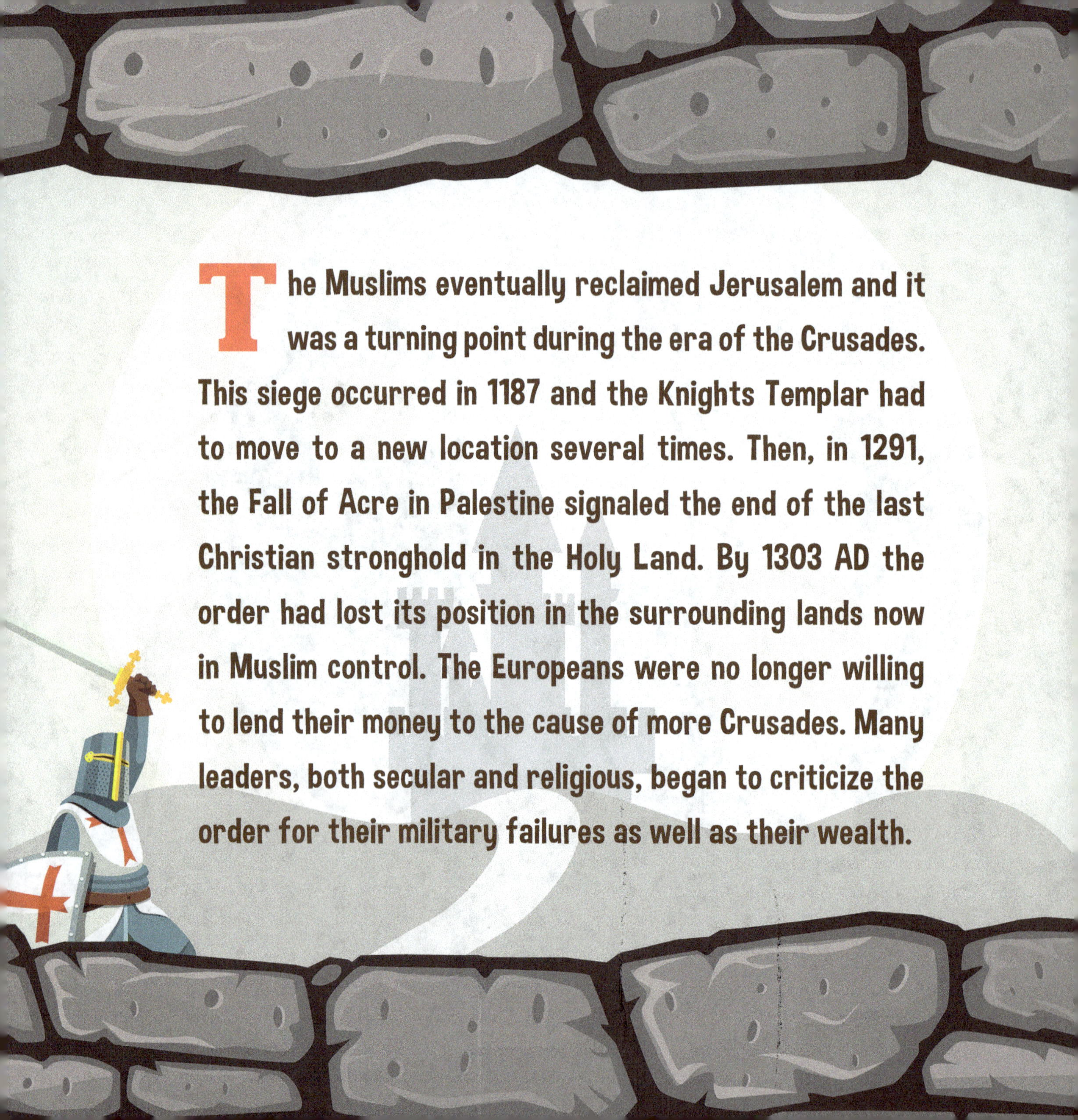

The Muslims eventually reclaimed Jerusalem and it was a turning point during the era of the Crusades. This siege occurred in 1187 and the Knights Templar had to move to a new location several times. Then, in 1291, the Fall of Acre in Palestine signaled the end of the last Christian stronghold in the Holy Land. By 1303 AD the order had lost its position in the surrounding lands now in Muslim control. The Europeans were no longer willing to lend their money to the cause of more Crusades. Many leaders, both secular and religious, began to criticize the order for their military failures as well as their wealth.

TEMPLARS DEFENDING
THEIR STRONGHOLD

KING PHILIP IV

When the Knights Templar moved their base of operations to Paris, France, they made an enemy of King Philip IV. The king was in debt and they wouldn't lend money to him any longer so he vowed he would bring their destruction.

EXECUTIONS OF THE
KNIGHTS TEMPLAR

JACQUES DE MOLAY

On the 13th of October in 1307, many of the Templars were captured including their Grand Master at that time, Jacques de Molay. They were unmercifully tortured until they confessed to charges that today historians believe were completely false. They included charges of heresy against the Church, worship of the devil, defiling the cross, and fraud and financial corruption.

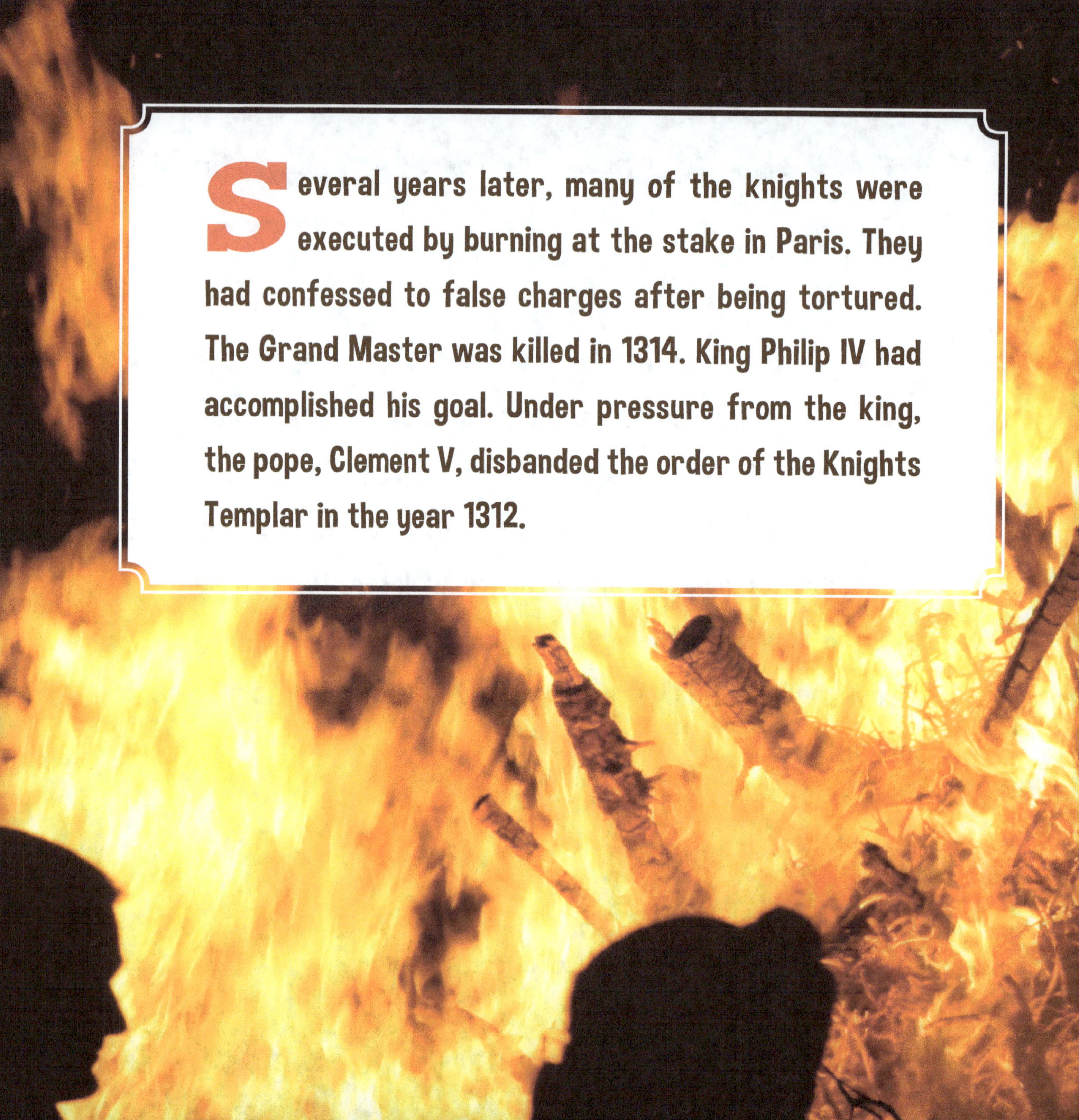

Several years later, many of the knights were executed by burning at the stake in Paris. They had confessed to false charges after being tortured. The Grand Master was killed in 1314. King Philip IV had accomplished his goal. Under pressure from the king, the pope, Clement V, disbanded the order of the Knights Templar in the year 1312.

Many of their properties and their wealth were handed off to their rivals, another order of knights called the Hospitallers. However, King Philip IV and the king of England, Edward II, are thought to have been responsible for seizing much of the Templars' wealth.

DO THE KNIGHTS TEMPLAR STILL EXIST?

The Catholic Church has stated that the torture of the Knights Templar was a mistake and that Pope Clement V succumbed to pressure by King Philip IV and other rulers. Most historians believe that this was the end of the order, but there are many people who disagree. They believe the order went underground.

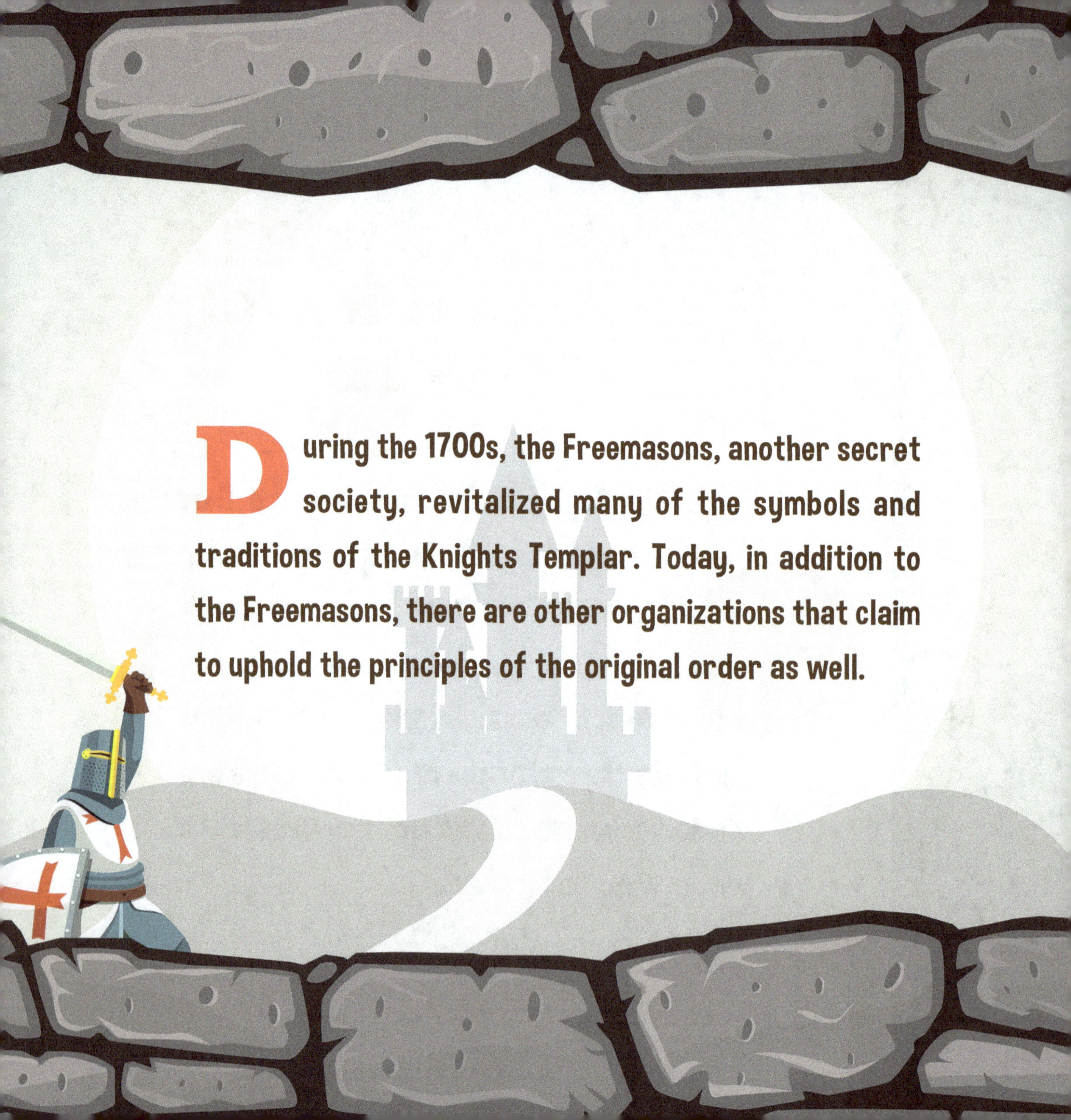

During the 1700s, the Freemasons, another secret society, revitalized many of the symbols and traditions of the Knights Templar. Today, in addition to the Freemasons, there are other organizations that claim to uphold the principles of the original order as well.

FREEMASON SYMBOL

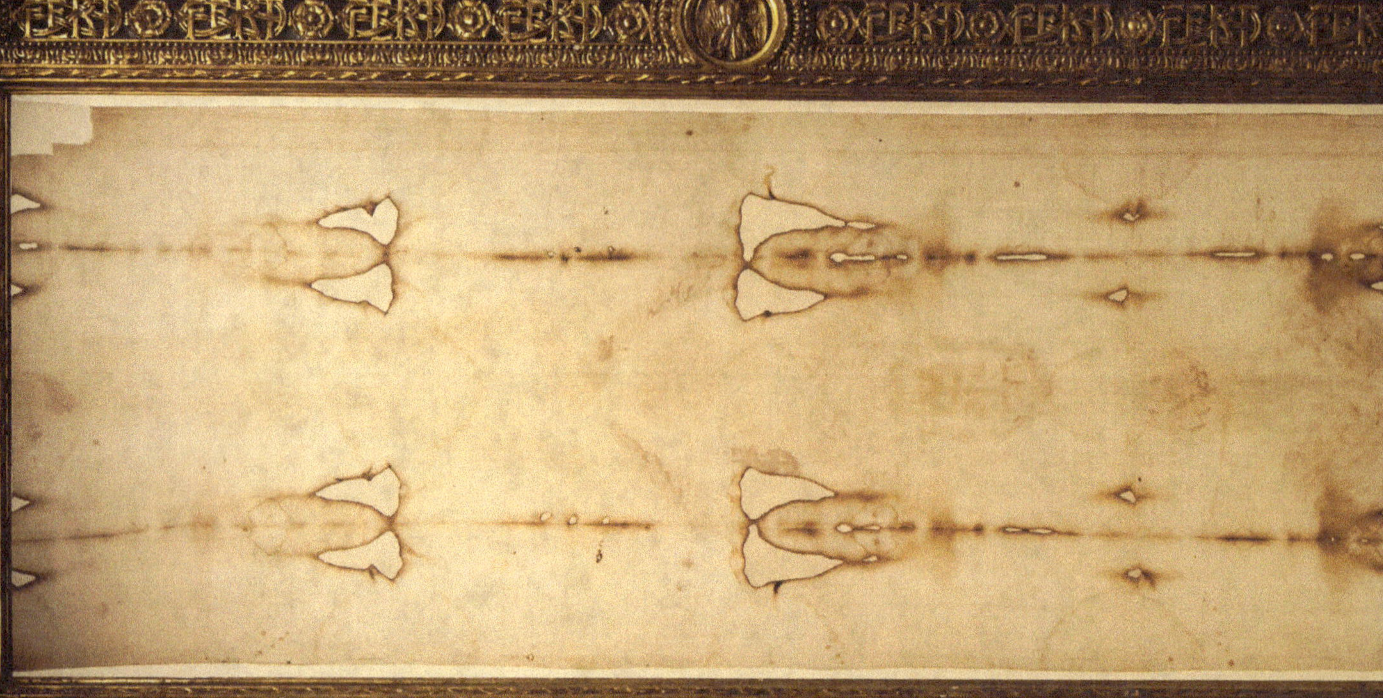

There are many mysterious stories that have surfaced in modern times about their secrets. Some believe that the Shroud of Turin, the linen cloth that was used to wrap Christ's body before it was buried and has an impression of Christ's face, was protected by the knights for centuries after the Crusades.

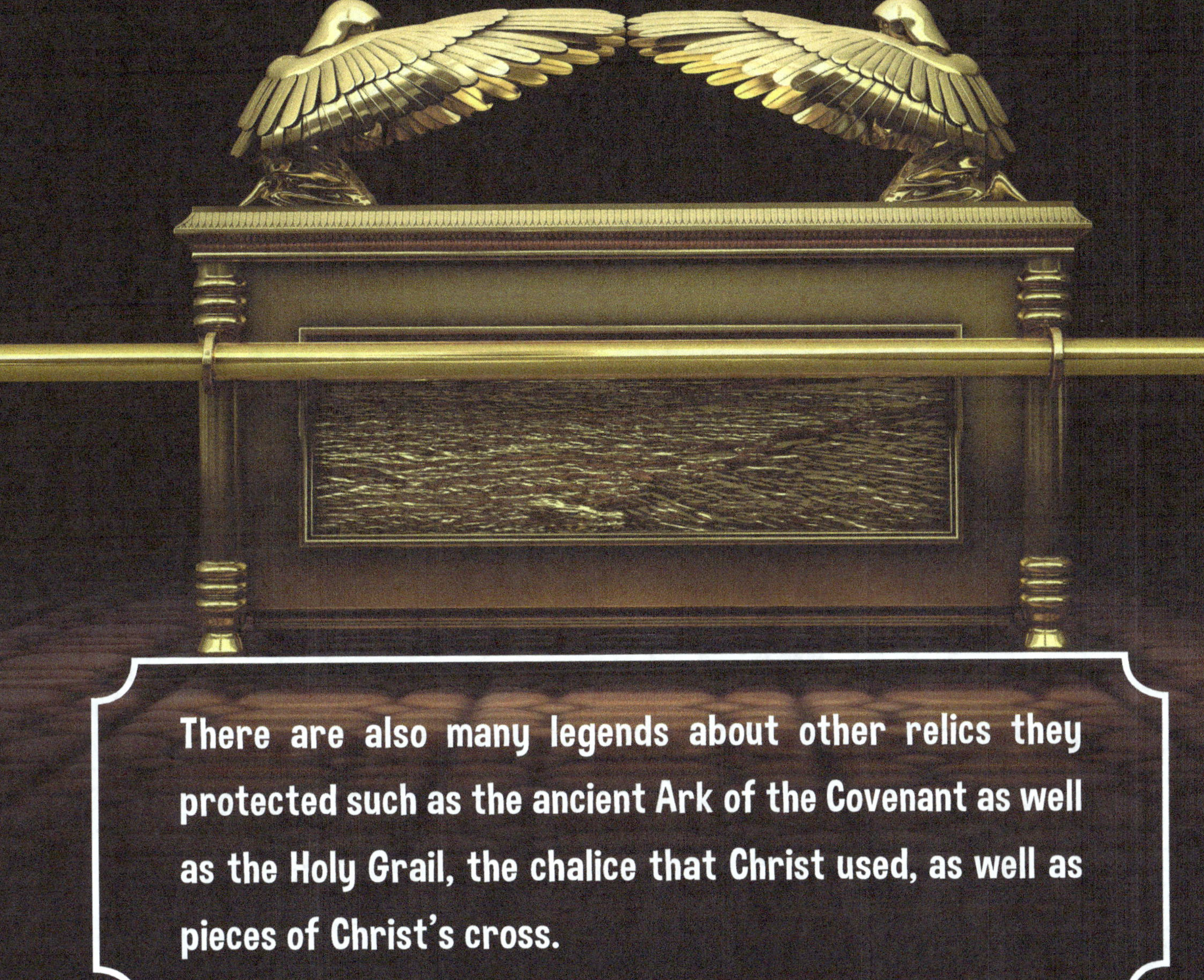

There are also many legends about other relics they protected such as the ancient Ark of the Covenant as well as the Holy Grail, the chalice that Christ used, as well as pieces of Christ's cross.

THE
DA VINCI
CODE
A NOVEL
DAN BROWN
AUTHOR OF ANGELS & DEMONS

In Dan Brown's book, The Da Vinci Code, he depicts the Knights Templar as protecting Christ's bloodline, although the Church believes that Christ never had children.

IN CONCLUSION..

The original mission of the order of the Knights Templar was to protect pilgrims on their journey through Muslim territories surrounding the regained Holy Land. Over time, their small band of knights grew in numbers, influence, and mystery.

Awesome! Now that you've read about the Knights Templar you may want to read more about Medieval times in the Baby Professor book *The Role of Religion and Divinity in the Middle Ages.*

Visit
BABY PROFESSOR
EDUCATION KIDS
www.BabyProfessorBooks.com
to download Free Baby Professor eBooks
and view our catalog of new and exciting
Children's Books